A MAN FOR ALL SEASONS

The Life of

George Washington Carver

Written by Stephen Krensky   Paintings by Wil Clay

Amistad

Collins

An Imprint of HarperCollins*Publishers*

Amistad and Collins are imprints of HarperCollins Publishers.

A Man for All Seasons
Text copyright © 2008 by Stephen Krensky
Paintings copyright © 2008 by Wil Clay

Manufactured in China.

Library of Congress Cataloging-in-Publication Data
Krensky, Stephen.
A man for all seasons / by Stephen Krensky ; illustrated by Wil Clay.
p.   cm.   Summary: Profiles the African American scientist George Washington Carver,
who not only put the peanut on the map, but was also one of the first advocates for recycling.
ISBN 978-0-06-027885-4 (trade bdg.) — ISBN 978-0-06-027886-1 (lib. bdg.)
1. Carver, George Washington, 1864?–1943—Juvenile literature. 2. African American
agriculturalists—Biography—Juvenile literature. 3. Agriculturalists—United States—
Biography—Juvenile literature. [1. Carver, George Washington, 1864?–1943.
2. Agriculturalists. 3. African Americans—Biography] I. Clay, Wil, ill. II. Title.
S417.C3 K74 2008   630'.92—dc21   [B]   2002020543   CIP   AC

Design by Rachel L. Schoenberg
1 2 3 4 5 6 7 8 9 10

First Edition

To Phoebe Yeh
—S.K.

To Alvin Cannon,
my neighbor who modeled
as the young George Carver
—W.C.

Young George Carver always liked gardens. He stuck his nose in the flowers and poked his fingers in the dirt. When a plant got sick, George figured out what would make it better. Sometimes a plant needed more water or sunshine. Other times it needed different dirt for its roots.

Nature was full of mystery—and surprises. Why did beetles attack potatoes but leave carrots alone? How did a small white seed become a big orange pumpkin? One day George brought home milkweed stalks so that he could watch the pods open. When they finally did, a blizzard of fluffy seeds filled the house. After that, George had to empty his pockets before he came inside.

George and his big brother, Jim, lived on the Carver farm in Diamond Grove, Missouri. Their father had died just before George was born in 1864, and their mother died only a few months after. The Carvers, Moses and Susan, owned the boys and their mother as slaves. They continued to raise them, though, even after the Civil War ended and slavery was abolished.

Jim grew up strong and eager. He often helped out Uncle Moses in the fields. George was smaller and sickly. He stayed near the house, where Aunt Susan taught him to cook and sew and tend the garden.

The Carvers taught the boys all they knew—to read and write and count. That was enough for Jim, but not George. The Carvers hired a tutor, but soon George was asking questions even the tutor couldn't answer. George would have liked to attend the town's one-room school, but only white children were allowed there. Sometimes George sat outside and listened to the lessons.

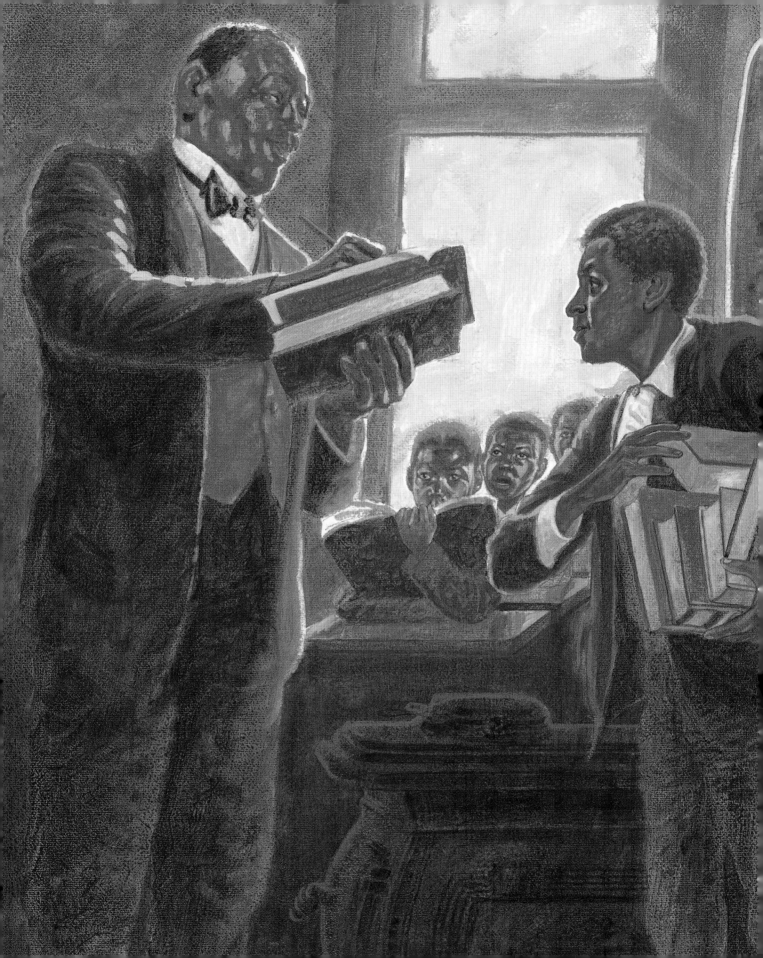

Eager to continue his education, George struck out on his own. At twelve he moved to Neosho, a nearby town with a more advanced school for blacks. George spent a year studying there, doing chores in return for room and board.

After that, he began traveling through Missouri and Kansas. He worked as a cook and a handyman while he continued his patchwork education. He wrote later, "I never saw anybody doing anything with his hands that I couldn't do with mine."

At one point George ran a laundry in Minneapolis, Kansas. By chance, another George Carver was living there, too. Sometimes orders got mixed up and sent to the wrong place. To avoid this confusion, George added a middle initial—a *W*—to his name. The *W* didn't stand for anything special at first. Then a friend remarked that George was so honest, he reminded her of George Washington. Delighted with the compliment, George began signing his name George Washington Carver.

George finally graduated from high school at twenty in 1884. His first attempt to enter a college that fall ended abruptly. Although his application had been accepted by mail, school officials turned him away upon his arrival when they discovered his skin wasn't white. This discrimination was not unusual. In many states black people could not eat in certain restaurants or sleep in certain hotels. On trains they sat in separate areas that were worn and dirty compared to where the white people sat.

Deeply discouraged, George put his education aside. He continued working here and there until he began farming in 1886. There was little wood on the Kansas plains, so he built his one-room house out of sod bricks. For three years he raised seventeen acres of corn and other crops. The winters were bitter cold and the summers blazing hot, but George managed to fit in some fun. In his spare moments, he collected rock samples, played the accordion at community dances, and took his first art classes.

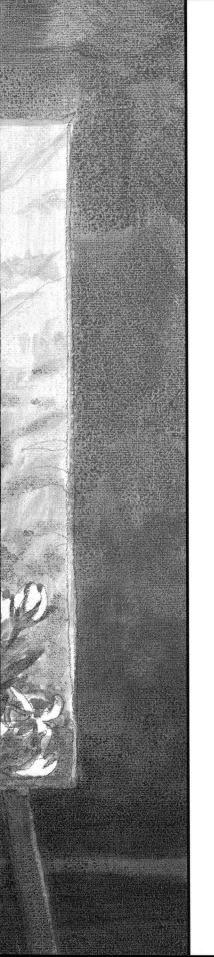

Around 1889, George gave up the farm and resumed his wandering. A year later he was living in Iowa, where his friends encouraged him to try college again. Following their advice, he enrolled at nearby Simpson College.

George studied painting at first. But he realized that a black man in America still could not hope to make a career in art. At his art teacher's suggestion, he transferred to Iowa Agricultural College. When Susan Carver asked him about college, he told her, "No man has enough learning, Aunt Sue, and me, I'm still trying to find out what makes it rain and why sunflowers grow so tall."

George was very busy at college. He studied techniques that helped plants grow stronger and healthier. One method was to take parts of two different plants and graft them together. A second was to cross-fertilize them—to take cells from one plant and mix them with those from another. He filled his free time with memberships in debating and agricultural clubs and became a trainer for the college football team.

It wasn't always easy, though, to concentrate on his work. Because George was the only black student, some people called him ugly names. He wasn't able to eat or live with the other students. Money also remained a concern, and George collected everything from cast-off clothes to pencil stubs to get by.

When George graduated in 1894, he was recognized as a promising botanist and invited to continue his work in a graduate program. His new responsibilities also included teaching freshman courses, something he very much enjoyed. As the first black graduate of a white college and its first black teacher, George began making a name for himself.

Important Events in the Life of George Washington Carver

1864	Born during the summer in Diamond Grove, Missouri (his father dies in a wagon accident before his birth)
1876	Leaves home to begin schooling in Neosho, Missouri
1883	Brother, Jim, dies of smallpox
1884	Graduates from high school in Minneapolis, Kansas
1890	Enters Simpson College, Indianola, Iowa
1891	Transfers to Iowa Agricultural College
1892	Exhibits a painting at the Chicago World's Fair
1894	Receives Bachelor of Agriculture degree from Iowa Agricultural College
1896	Receives Master of Agriculture degree from Iowa Agricultural College
	Begins teaching at the Tuskegee Institute in Alabama
1916	Elected Fellow of the Royal Society for the Encouragement of Arts, London, England
1921	Speaks before Congress on behalf of peanut growers
1923	Receives Spingarn Medal for Distinguished Service to Science from the National Association for the Advancement of Colored People (NAACP)
1928	Receives Honorary Doctor of Science degree, Simpson College
1920s–30s	Corresponds with automobile maker Henry Ford, inventor Thomas Edison, and Indian leader Mahatma Gandhi, among others
1938	Receives Roosevelt Medal for outstanding contribution to Southern agriculture
1941	George Washington Carver Museum opens at Tuskegee Institute
1943	Dies on January 5
	Congress creates the George Washington Carver National Monument, Diamond Grove, Missouri

As the years passed, Carver's fame grew. Farmers from all over wrote him, asking questions. Many people would gladly have paid him for his help, but he refused to consider it. "If I know the answer," he wrote, "you can have it for the price of a postage stamp. The Lord charges me nothing for knowledge, and I will charge you the same."

He also traveled widely, giving speeches about his research. Even fame, though, did not free Carver from prejudice and embarrassment. In some public dining rooms, he was not permitted to eat at a dinner where he was the main speaker. Or he was forced to enter through a hotel's back entrance because blacks were not allowed in at the front.

Some younger black leaders were disappointed in Carver's silence over these issues. They wanted him to be angry and strong, to use his position to take a bolder stand for civil rights.

But that was not Carver's way. His energy fueled his work, not his anger. Certainly the insults bothered him. But it was more important to reach a greater audience. As he once wrote, "The primary idea in all my work was to help the farmer and fill the poor man's empty dinner pail."

George Washington Carver spent his whole life fostering his love of growing things. Unlike others who tried to conquer nature with chemicals and pesticides, Carver viewed nature as his partner. He took equal pleasure in a beautiful rose and the hundreds of uses he devised for the peanut.

Long before his death in 1943, farmers and scientists, including many of his former students, began furthering his work. Today, finding natural solutions to natural problems and recycling one industry's waste product into other useful forms are ideas we take for granted. With this legacy George Washington Carver truly accomplished the greatest good for the greatest number, not only for black people, but for everyone else as well.

Carver especially liked the peanut. It was easy to grow and very nutritious. He created dozens of new things from it—peanut milk, peanut flour, even peanut-skin cream.

Convincing other people of the peanut's potential was difficult. One night Professor Carver invited a group of businessmen to a grand dinner. These people had money to invest in new products and ideas. Carver prepared the food himself—soup, chicken, bread, and ice cream. As they ate together, the men applauded Carver and his cooking skills.

Carver smiled. Then he revealed the truth. Every dish in the whole meal contained peanuts. His guests were amazed. Perhaps this peanut business had promise after all.

Carver cooked up other surprises, too. He repeatedly tried grinding or squeezing or shredding plants and vegetables into different forms. Powdered peanut shells, he discovered, could be pressed into paper. And stringy sweet potatoes made a fine base for useful soaps and glue.

Almost always he worked alone on old equipment in his lab. While investigating a new idea, Carver often forgot to eat or sleep. Keeping records, attending meetings, and making schedules were not his strengths. Sometimes he didn't even remember to cash his own paychecks.

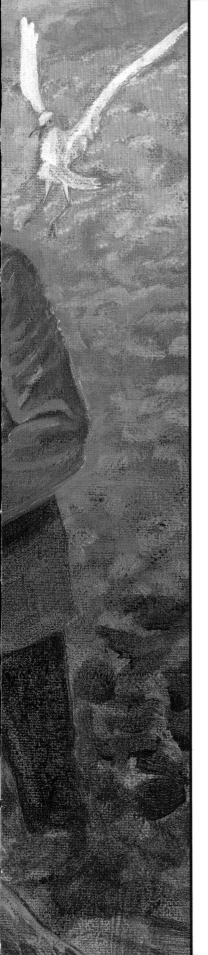

Carver also encouraged his students to be creative. When he discovered that the institute lacked money for classroom equipment, he led his students to the town dump. There they collected rusty pans, dusty bottles, and other reusable trash.

Back at school, Carver cut down the bottles into beakers and flasks. He reshaped the scraps of tin into strainers and spatulas. He patiently untangled knots of string and rolled them up neatly for future use. When he was done, he had the makings of a simple laboratory.

All around Tuskegee lived poor black farmers who could benefit from Carver's teachings. These former slaves and their children had little money. They swapped the use of land and tools for a large share of their crops.

To reach these sharecroppers, Professor Carver and his students took wagons of food and supplies up the backcountry roads. In his high-pitched, soft voice, Carver explained that dirt was like a living thing. It got hungry and thirsty, needing both fertilizers and water to stay healthy.

Few of the farmers listened at first. They were superstitious about growing things and suspicious of change. Growing cotton was all they knew. Carver persisted, explaining that over time fields became tired from growing only one thing. He told the farmers to rotate their crops, planting cowpeas or sweet potatoes or peanuts. If they didn't, soon nothing at all would grow on the land.